GLUTEI
SLOW CI
COOKBuuK

The 50 Best Ever Recipes For
Unforgettable Healthy Meals

SOFIA DAVIS

Table of Contents

My Struggle With Gluten

Why is it that there are so many people suffering from gluten intolerance or allergy? There are thousands and thousands of people, both grown-ups and children, struggling with it every day.

And I'm one of them!

Ever since I was a kid my parents noticed unusual reactions every time I had pasta or bread – stomach problems were just a few of them. But the moment they noticed that I was losing weight they began to worry and decided to look further into it, as it was affecting me more and more.

After many tests, the diagnosis came – gluten intolerance. My parents were frightened, mainly because it was something new to them. They had never had serious health problems. All the unknowns were scary.

Luckily, they stood strong, looked for as much information as possible, and before I knew it, I was being introduced to a brand new diet.

I have to admit, though, I hated it back then. Try as hard as she might, the new food that mom made me eat was not appealing at all and she had a hard time finding recipes, poor thing!

But as I grew up, I understood that my condition is something I have to get along with rather than fight against. And that is what I did, and this is how this book was born – from experience and tried and tested recipes!

My hope is that the information in this book helps you get through the gluten-free struggle a little bit more easily than

I did. There's everything here, including informative background info on gluten allergies and intolerances, tips on how to choose a slow cooker and, of course, 50 mouthwateringly delicious recipes that you simply won't be able to resist!

It's not easy, but it's not impossible either. Think of it as a challenge and you will make it through!

Plus, the technology we have on hand nowadays makes our job even easier – and here, of course, I'm talking about slow cookers, also known as crock pots. The idea behind slow cookers is that no time is wasted in order to cook something delicious. Simply put all the ingredients in the crock pot and turn it on. That's all you have to do, literally! No mixing is required, no supervising, the slow cooker will do its job all alone and the final result will be beyond expectations.

It's easy, simple and perfect for the modern person, balancing time between work, family and friends, whilst also having to deal with a gluten intolerance or allergy.

Enjoy!

Gluten Intolerance vs. Gluten Allergy

Before we get started, let's clarify the difference between a gluten intolerance and a gluten allergy. Many people tend to mistake them for one another but the only thing they have in common is the gluten. The reactions they cause and their effects are very different.

Gluten intolerance is a condition that causes a person to react after eating gluten – a protein found in wheat, barley and rye. Ingesting gluten can lead to stomach problems, joint pain, fatigue, depression and weight loss. Experts get to this diagnosis after ruling out a gluten allergy or the Celiac disease. Gluten intolerance is not as bad as an allergy, but it definitely affects the body if no measures are taken.

When it comes to gluten allergies, the reactions are far more severe and can take place in a matter of minutes, sometimes threatening life. In the case of an allergy, the body sees the gluten as an intruder and quickly reacts to it. This leads to irritated skin, rashes, swollen skin, bad stomach problems and the list goes on. The allergy can only be treated with medication if it happens, and if the reactions are severe an emergency intervention may be needed.

Currently, the only treatment for gluten intolerance is through diet and lifestyle. Only a diet excluding all sources of gluten can show an improvement in the condition.

The Diet – What to Eat and What to Avoid

There is nothing more important in a gluten-free diet than the food you are eating and the ingredients you are using when cooking. That's why having a clear list of what to eat and what to avoid is crucial.

What to Eat
- Grains that do not contain gluten: corn (corn flour, corn meal, grits), rice (whit, brown, basmati), amaranth, buckwheat, millet, quinoa, teff, sorghum and soy
- Dairy products – milk, cheese, yogurt
- Healthy oils – canola, coconut, olive oil
- Fruits and vegetables
- Meat and seafood
- Eggs
- Nuts, beans and legumes
- Arrowroot, cornstarch, potato starch
- Spices
- Oats – pure oats are gluten free, unless they've been contaminated. Read the label before buying

What to Avoid
- Wheat in any form, including spelt, durum, semolina, couscous or cake flour, but also wheat starch, barley, malt and malt vinegar
- Rye
- Store bought floured meat, unless stated on the package that is gluten free
- Beer because usually is fermented from barley, unless stated otherwise

The Benefits of a Gluten Free Diet

With more and more people suffering from either gluten free intolerance or allergy, the gluten free diet has become more and more popular. You may have noticed that more and more products wear the label "Gluten Free" on the shelves of big stores.

Gluten is a protein found in wheat, certain grains and cereals. The purpose of gluten is to bring elasticity into many products, such as bread and other types of dough. Gluten is developed by kneading or mixing until the mixture becomes elastic. This process is crucial in bread because it yields a fluffy, well risen, flaky bread, but it's just as important in cakes or cupcakes.

Improved Digestion

Gluten intolerance usually leads to stomach problems and inefficient absorption of nutrients. It gets even worse for those with the Celiac disease because this disorder causes inflammation in the small intestine as well as flattening of the intestinal villi which drastically reduces the absorption of nutrients, leading to malnutrition. A gluten free diet reduces stomach upset, diarrhea, gas, abdominal cramps, bloating and constipation.

Improves General Health

Gluten Intolerance often causes headaches, foggy thinking and even depression, but a change to a diet without gluten can fix that.

Inflammation

People with gluten intolerance may experience joint pain, muscle cramps or numb legs, but a diet without gluten helps reduce inflammation and reliefs the pain.

Improves Eczema

Both intolerance and allergy can lead to skin rashes or even eczema. Being gluten free improves the eczema and reliefs rashes.

Boosts Energy

Being sensitive to gluten means that the nutrients found in the food aren't absorbed as they should, therefore the energy level is low. Changing your diet leads to boosted energy and a strong body.

Slow Cooker – Advantages

Slow cookers are being used more and more nowadays, for a very good reason! Let's look at some of the advantages crock pots have:

- The long cooking time allows flavors to develop, creating complex dishes.
- Saves time and money – using a slow cooker doesn't take much preparation and usually only requires chopping some ingredients and mixing them together, turning on the crock pot on and letting it do its job.
- Allows pre-preparation – you can get all the ingredients ready the night before then turn it on when you leave for work.
- It allows you to cook tougher pieces of meat, such as chock roast or stew beef. This also saves you money.
- Having a slow cooker means the stove and oven are free to use for side dishes or anything else you want to cook.
- You can leave the slow cooker unattended all day while you can do other things, from spending time with the family to shopping or time for yourself. However, before leaving it unattended, be sure to observe it once on both low and high settings just to make sure it's working properly.
- You don't have to add oil to a slow cooker and that allows for healthier cooking. Feel free to also trim the fat off the meat.
- Because slow cookers have a lid that's sealed on, the liquid won't evaporate so you don't have to use as much liquid as a recipe cooked on the stove.

- Since the liquid is not evaporating, sauces won't thicken unless you add a thickener. Consider that when cooking stews for instance.

How to Choose a Slow Cooker

Before buying a slow cooker, you need to ask yourself a few questions, then decide which brand or size is the best for you.

How many people are you cooking for?
- 2 quart slow cookers are best for breakfast or for single servings
- 3 ½ quarts is suited for 2-3 servings
- 4 quart slow cooker will feed 2 and have leftovers for the next day or feed 4
- 5 quart is better for 5 or 6
- 6 quart or more is suitable for a bigger family, unless you want to cook ahead of time then freeze in individual portions for later serving.

Manual or programmable?
Manual ones are cheaper, but they can't be programmed to automatically switch on or off when you want to. That's why I recommend buying a programmable one, because eventually the slightly higher investment you make will be recovered in time saved!

Recipes

International Favorites

Greek Style Chicken

Prep time: 10 minutes
Cook time: 6 ½ hours
Serves: 4

This chicken reminds me of the refreshing flavor or Greece, the sun, the good quality olive oil and all the flavors of the Greek islands. You will love this tender dish if you like salty food.

What to expect

The intense aroma of the garlic makes an excellent team with a touch of basil and the tanginess of the lemon juice. These flavors infuse the meat, making it fragrant and tender, absolutely delicious.

Ingredients:
4 chicken breasts
3 garlic cloves, minced
2 tablespoons lemon juice
3 tablespoons extra virgin olive oil
6 basil leaves, finely chopped
1 pinch freshly ground black pepper
Salt to taste

Directions:
Combine the garlic, lemon juice, olive oil and basil. Spread the mixture over the chicken meat and place them all in your slow cooker. Cover the pot with its lid and cook on low settings for 6 ½ hours or until the meat is tender. Serve the chicken with your favorite side dish.

Chicken Cacciatore

Prep time: 10 minutes
Cook time: 7 ½ hours
Serves: 6

This Italian dish is a real delight for those loving Mediterranean flavors. But even if it's your first encounter with these flavors, this recipe is surely worth a try!

<u>What to expect</u>

Expect a creamy and rich dish that brings out the best of the chicken meat. The sauce is fresh, loaded with flavor while the meat is perfectly complemented by the tangy tomatoes and sweet bell peppers.

Ingredients:
1 pound chicken meat, cubed
1 pound mushrooms, sliced
1 large onion, finely chopped
2 red bell peppers, cored and diced
1 carrot, diced
¼ cup red wine
1 cup tomato puree
½ teaspoon dried thyme
½ teaspoon dried basil
½ teaspoon dried oregano
1 bay leaf
Salt, pepper to taste

Directions:
Combine the chicken with the mushrooms in your crock pot. Stir in the rest of the ingredients then season with salt and freshly ground pepper. Cover the pot with its lid and cook on low settings for 7 ½ hours. Serve the chicken warm.

Italian Caponata

Prep time: 15 minutes
Cook time: 4 ½ hours
Servings: 6

Caponata is a simple, rustic Sicilian dish that relies on natural sweetness of vegetables to create a delicious meal that can be served either as a main dish or a side dish.

<u>What to expect</u>

The Mediterranean flavors found in this dish are what make it special. The dried herbs preserve the same intense aroma as fresh herbs and you have the freedom to use any of them.

Ingredients:
1 pound ripe tomatoes, sliced
2 zucchinis, cubed
2 eggplants, cubed
1 celery stalk, sliced
1 red onion, sliced
2 teaspoons dried oregano
4 tablespoons extra virgin olive oil
1 teaspoon sea salt
½ teaspoon freshly ground pepper

Directions:
Mix the vegetables in your crock pot. Sprinkle with dried oregano, salt and pepper then drizzle with olive oil. Cover the pot with its lid and cook on high settings for 4 ½ hours. Serve the caponata warm or chilled.

Beef Ragu

Prep time: 15 minutes
Cook time: 9 hours
Serves: 10

Ragu is a well-known Italian sauce, used for both pasta and lasagna. It is usually made with a mix of pork and beef, but this recipe uses only beef because it's looking for the delicate aroma of the beef before anything else.

What to expect

Ragu is a universal sauce and what makes it special is the long cooking time that allows the flavor to develop properly, creating a rich flavored sauce, thick and delicious.

Ingredients:
2 pounds ground beef meat
3 onions, chopped
4 garlic cloves, chopped
1 pound baby carrots
4 ripe tomatoes, peeled and diced
1 cup tomato puree
1 bay leaf
1 teaspoon dried basil
1 teaspoon dried oregano
1 teaspoon dried marjoram
Salt, pepper to taste

Directions:
Place the meat in a crock pot then add the rest of the ingredients. Season with salt and freshly ground pepper then cook the ragu on low settings for 9 hours or until the sauce is flavorful and rich. At this point, you can either serve it

with pasta or use it in lasagna or other similar dishes, but you can also freeze it in individual portions to use later.

Asian Pork with Noodles

Prep time: 20 minutes
Cook time: 4 ½ hours
Serves: 10

Yes, noodles can be made in a crock pot, but you have to add them closer to the end of the cooking time to ensure they don't tear apart while cooking.

What to expect

It's a light and yet filling meal, loaded with Asian flavors and absolutely delicious if you're a fan of such flavors. Ginger, hoisin sauce and green onions are just a few of the most intense flavors of the dish.

Ingredients:
2 pounds lean pork tenderloin, cubed
1 tablespoon hoisin sauce
1 teaspoon brown sugar
1 teaspoon grated ginger
4 garlic cloves, chopped
1 teaspoon sesame oil
2 carrots cut in small sticks
1 celery stalk, sliced
1 cup vegetable stock
16 oz. dried rice noodles
4 green onions
¼ cup chopped cilantro
¼ cup chopped parsley
2 limes, juiced
Salt, pepper to taste

Directions:

Combine the meat with the hoisin sauce, brown sugar, ginger, garlic, sesame oil, carrots, celery, salt and pepper in your crock pot. Add the stock. Cover with a lid and cook on high settings for 4 ½ hours.
½ hours before the time is up, add the noodles, green onions, cilantro and parsley.
Serve the noodles warm.

Slow Cooker Paella

Prep time: 15 minutes
Cook time: 4 ½ hours
Serves: 8

Paella has Spanish roots and its staple is the use of various types of meat to create a complex dish, very filling and nutritious.

<u>What to expect</u>

The main flavorings of this recipe are the three types of meat: the spicy, garlicky sausages, the delicate chicken breasts and the delicious shrimps. Turmeric is added for color and paprika for heat and the final result is a one of a kind dish.

Ingredients:
1 ½ cups brown rice
3 cups vegetable stock
1 onion, chopped
1 green bell pepper, cored and diced
1 red pepper, seeded and chopped
4 garlic cloves, chopped
1 pound chicken sausages, cubed
2 chicken breasts, cubed
1 pound fresh shrimps, peeled and deveined
2 cups canned diced tomatoes
1 teaspoon smoked paprika
½ teaspoon turmeric
2 cups frozen green peas
Salt, pepper to taste

Directions:

Combine the vegetables with the rice, stock, chicken sausages and chicken breasts. Add the turmeric, paprika and green peas then season with salt and pepper and cook on high settings for 4 ½ hours. 30 minutes before the cooking time is up, throw in the shrimps and finish cooking. Serve the paella warm.

Thai Chicken Soup

Prep time: 15 minutes
Cook time: 6 ½ hours
Serves: 10

A bowl of soup is always welcomed after a long day at work, isn't it?! You will find it very soothing and its flavors will relax you spoon after spoon.

<u>What to expect</u>

This soup has an intense Thai aroma, but it's not overwhelming at all. The coconut milk, curry paste and fish sauce are very subtle touches and really enhance the aroma of all the other ingredients.

Ingredients:
2 tablespoons curry paste
2 cans coconut milk
2 cups chicken stock
2 tablespoon fish sauce
1 tablespoon brown sugar
4 chicken breasts, cubed
1 onion, chopped
3 garlic cloves, chopped
2 red bell peppers, cored and diced
1 lime, juiced
Salt, pepper to taste
¼ cup chopped cilantro

Directions:
Combine the coconut milk with the curry paste and chicken stock in your crock pot. Stir in the fish sauce, brown sugar, chicken, onion, garlic and bell pepper then add salt and

pepper. Cook on low settings for 6 ½ hours. When done, stir in the lime juice and cilantro then serve the soup warm.

Main Dishes

Crustless Quiche

Prep time: 15 minutes
Cook time: 6 hours
Serves: 8

Quiche is the mix between a tart and an omelet. More
specifically, usually it has a buttery crust and an egg filling,
but this particular recipe is different because it has no crust
and it's incredibly easy to make.

<u>What to expect</u>

It's a rich dish which can be served for both lunch and
dinner, but it works great as breakfast as well. It's a fairly
basic dish but it will surprise you with its deliciousness.

Ingredients:
8 eggs
1 cup heavy cream
2 cups fresh spinach, shredded
1 ½ cups crumbled feta cheese
4 basil leaves, shredded
1 shallot, sliced
1 garlic clove, chopped
4 chicken sausages, cut in smaller pieces
Salt, pepper to taste

Directions:
Beat the eggs with the heavy cream. Add salt and pepper
then stir in the spinach, feta cheese, basil, shallot and garlic.
Add the chicken sausages as well then pour the mixture into

your slow cooker and cook on low settings for 6 hours or until set. Slice and serve the quiche warm.

Chicken Pot Roast

Prep time: 20 minutes
Cook time: 7 ¼ hours
Serves: 8

This is a classic dish, filling and delicious, that makes an excellent lunch or dinner. You can even freeze individual portions and serve them later after reheating.

What to expect

In terms of flavors, this dish is quite delicate. Nothing stands out and yet, the dish is balanced and highly flavorful, absolutely delicious.

Ingredients:
1 whole chicken, cut in smaller pieces
2 carrots, sliced
2 celery stalks, sliced
4 red potatoes, peeled and cubed
½ cup small onions, peeled
½ teaspoon dried oregano
Salt, pepper to taste
2 tablespoons cornstarch
1 cup chicken stock
1 bay leaf

Directions:
Mix the meat with salt and pepper to taste then sprinkle with flour and toss around to evenly coat the flour. Place the meat in the crock pot. Add the vegetables, dried oregano, bay leaf then pour in the stock and cook the pot pie in the crock pot on low settings for 7 ¼ hours. Serve warm.

Garlicky Chicken

Prep time: 15 minutes
Cook time: 7 hours
Serves: 8

Chicken is a forgiving kind of meat and it can be combined with most vegetables. Garlic is a great choice and it gives so much flavors. You will love this garlicky chicken bite after bite.

<u>What to expect</u>

Despite having plenty of garlic, the final dish is balanced and the garlic taste is not overwhelming for the taste buds. Instead, the chicken proves to be a delicious piece of meat, amazing served with potatoes or another mild side dish.

Ingredients:
4 chicken breasts, halved
2 tablespoons olive oil
1 teaspoon dried basil
1 teaspoon dried oregano
10 garlic cloves, peeled but left whole
Salt, pepper to taste

Directions:
Sprinkle the meat with the dried herbs, salt and pepper and place the meat in your crock pot. Add the garlic cloves and drizzle with olive oil. Cover the pot with its lid and cook on low settings for 7 hours. Serve the chicken warm. If you want, you can mash the garlic and make a gravy using it as a base.

Beef and Vegetable Roast

Prep time: 15 minutes
Cook time: 9 hours
Serves: 8

The long cooking time leads to a very tender meat that literally melts in your mouth. The vegetables are just as tender and flavorful, absolutely delicious.

What to expect

You got to love the tenderness of the meat combined with the flavorful vegetables and the delicious juices they release in the pan. Feel free to add other vegetables if you prefer though.

Ingredients:
2 pounds beef meat, cubed
2 carrots, sliced
4 potatoes, peeled and cubed
1 pound cauliflower, cut into florets
1 onion, sliced
2 ripe tomatoes, sliced
4 garlic cloves, sliced
2 tablespoons olive oil
Salt, pepper to taste

Directions:
Mix the beef meat with the vegetables. Add salt and pepper to taste then drizzle with olive oil. Cover the crock pot with its lid and cook on low heat for 9 hours or until the meat is tender. Serve the beef warm.

BBQ Pork Ribs

Prep time: 2 hours
Cook time: 9 ½ hours
Serves: 8

How can you not love pork ribs?! Especially when they're as juicy and sticky as these?!

<u>What to expect</u>

This recipe is surely not avoiding heat and spiciness. In fact, that is the interesting thing about this recipe – it's both spicy and tempered and it makes you want for more once you had the first bite.

Ingredients:
4 pounds pork short ribs
½ cup BBQ sauce
1 teaspoon smoked paprika
½ teaspoon dried oregano
½ teaspoon dried basil
½ cup red wine
Salt, pepper to taste

Directions:
Combine the short ribs with the ketchup, paprika, oregano, basil and red wine. Add salt and pepper to taste and marinade the pork ribs for 1-2 hours or even overnight if you have time for it.
Transfer the pork ribs into the crock pot and cover with a lid. Cook on low settings for 9 ½ hours or until the meat is tender. Serve them warm.

Sage and Tomato Turkey
Prep time: 15 minutes
Cook time: 8 hours
Serves: 12

Turkey is one of the healthiest kinds of meat. It has little fat, low cholesterol and a very mild taste. Combined with sage and tomatoes, it yields a very delicious dish that can be served by the entire family.

What to expect

How can you not love this tender sage flavored meat, paired with the tangy tomatoes?! You will find these flavors quite surprising and the dish itself is one of the best ways to make the best of the turkey meat.

Ingredients:
1 turkey breast
4 garlic cloves, minced
2 tablespoons chopped parsley
2 tablespoons chopped cilantro
1 tablespoon dried sage
½ cup softened butter
1 tablespoon Worcestershire sauce
4 red potatoes, peeled and cubed
4 sweet potatoes, peeled and cubed
Salt, pepper to taste

Directions:
Mix the butter with the garlic, parsley, cilantro, sage and sauce. Spread the herbed butter over the turkey breast then place the meat in your crock pot. Arrange the potatoes around the meat and cover the pot with its lid. Cook for 8 hours on low settings then serve the dish warm.

BBQ Pulled Pork
Prep time: 15 minutes
Cook time: 10 hours
Serves: 6

Pulled pork is the kind of dish that can be served with anything, from sandwiches to burritos or even served with just mashed potatoes or roasted vegetables.

What to expect

Is a simple dish and the flavors are exposed – the spicy BBQ sauce and the heat of the chiles are the most powerful but they tone down the fatty pork meat and the final result is a dish that melts in your mouth bite after bite.

Ingredients:
2 pounds pork meat, cubed
2 teaspoons chipotle powder
2 tablespoons olive oil
2 poblano chiles, chopped
½ cup BBQ sauce
1 cup green chile salsa
Salt, pepper to taste

Directions:
Combine the meat with the chipotle powder, olive oil, chiles, BBQ sauce and salsa in your crock pot. Add salt and pepper to taste and cook the pork in your crock pot on low settings for 10 hours. When done, shred the meat with a fork and serve simple or in sandwiches.

Slow Cooker Spiced Ham

Prep time: 15 minutes
Cook time: 8 hours
Serves: 6-8

Ham is a very versatile dish. You can serve it simple, after you make it or slice it and serve it in sandwiches. It's tender and absolutely delicious.

What to expect

The spices used infuse the ham with an intense flavor, but they actually work with the smoky ham. The long cooking time yields a tender ham that can easily be shredded or sliced.

Ingredients:
1 piece of bone-in picnic ham
¼ cup brown sugar
2 teaspoons cumin powder
1 teaspoon smoked paprika
1 teaspoons ground coriander
1 teaspoon ground ginger
2 tablespoons balsamic vinegar

Directions:
Combine the brown sugar with the paprika, ground coriander, cumin, ginger and balsamic vinegar. Spread this mixture over the ham and rub it well into the ham. Place the ham in the crock pot and cover with its lid. Cook on low settings for 8 hours until the ham is tender. Slice or shred to serve.

Tender Beef and Caramelized Onions

Prep time: 15 minutes
Cook time: 7 hours
Serves: 8

Beef is great for slow cookers because it usually needs a long coking time, therefore it won't tear apart in the slow cooker. And the caramelized onion is a bold move for those loving the combination of sweet and salty.

What to expect

When caramelized, the onions turn rather sweet, but that is when the red wine interferes, balancing the flavor display perfectly into a dish that you won't forget any time soon. Add the earthy aroma of mushrooms and you've got a complete, delicious meal.

Ingredients:
2 pounds beef meat, cubed
4 large red onions, sliced
2 tablespoons olive oil
2 garlic cloves, chopped
1 tablespoon Worcestershire sauce
½ cup red wine
1 pound mushrooms, sliced
Salt, pepper to taste

Directions:
Heat the olive oil in a skillet and stir in the onions. Sauté for 15 minutes then transfer in a slow cooker. Stir in the beef, garlic, Worcestershire sauce, red wine and mushrooms. Season with salt and pepper and cook in your slow cooker for 7 hours on low settings.

Roasted Whole Chicken

Prep time: 10 minutes
Cook time: 8 ½ hours
Serves: 8

Using a slow cooker for cooking doesn't mean you have to give up on roasted chicken. Quite the opposite actually since a slow cooker can usually fit in a whole chicken. There's nothing stopping you!

What to expect

The recipe may be a basic one, cut the flavor display is quite amazing. The tangy lemon, the fragrant rosemary and the delicate basil – all combined into a delicious and juicy piece of chicken.

Ingredients:
1 whole chicken
1 teaspoon lemon zest
2 tablespoons lemon juice
4 garlic cloves, minced
1 teaspoon smoked paprika
1 teaspoon dried basil
1 tablespoon dried rosemary
2 teaspoons salt
½ teaspoon freshly ground pepper

Directions:
Mix the lemon zest, lemon juice, garlic, paprika, basil, rosemary, salt and pepper. Spread the mixture over the whole chicken, rubbing it well into the skin. Place the chicken into your crock pot and cook on low settings for 8 ½ hours.

Side Dishes

Spinach and Roasted Bell Pepper Casserole

Prep time: 15 minutes
Cook time: 4 hours
Serves: 8

Such a simple recipes and yet so delicious! You would
never think to combine bell peppers with chickpeas, but you
will love the sweetness of the dish.

What to expect

The flavors are quite simple and basic, but the outcome is
truly delicious and definitely worthy to be on your dinner
table.

Ingredients:
2 cups canned cannellini beans, drained
2 cups chickpeas, drained
4 basil leaves, chopped
1 shallot, chopped
6 canned roasted bell peppers, drained and chopped
4 cups shredded spinach
2 cups shredded mozzarella cheese
Salt, pepper to taste

Directions:
Mix the beans with the chickpeas, basil, shallot, bell
peppers and spinach. Add salt and pepper to taste and cover
the crock pot with its lid. Cook on high heat for 4 ½ hours.
30 minutes before the time is off, add the cheese and finish
cooking until the cheese is melted. It is better served warm.

Sweet Potato and Carrot Sauté

Prep time: 15 minutes
Cook time: 4 hours
Serves: 6

This recipe certainly goes on the sweeter side when it comes to flavorings and for that reason it works great as a side dish for steaks or salty, consistent dishes.

<u>What to expect</u>

As I said, it is a rather sweet side dish since both the sweet potatoes and carrots have a natural sweetness, but this sweetness works great with the spices added to create an amazing side dish.

Ingredients:
2 pounds sweet potatoes, peeled and cubed
1 pound baby carrots
½ cup orange juice
1 teaspoon dried sage
½ teaspoon dried thyme
½ teaspoon cumin seeds
2 bacon slices, chopped
Salt, pepper to taste

Directions:
Combine the sweet potatoes and baby carrots in a slow cooker. Pour in the orange juice then add the dried sage, thyme, cumin seeds and chopped bacon. Add salt and pepper to taste and cook the dish on high settings for 4 hours. Serve warm.

Balsamic Vinegar Vegetables

Prep time: 10 minutes
Cook time: 8 hours
Serves: 6

Roasted vegetables and a touch of tangy balsamic vinegar –
doesn't it sound delicious?! I sure love the sound of it!

<u>What to expect</u>

The natural sweetness of the vegetables is well balanced by
the tanginess of the balsamic vinegar so the final side dish is
absolutely delicious, perfect with any main dish you might
think of.

Ingredients:
2 zucchinis, sliced
2 carrots, sliced
1 eggplant, cubed
2 red potatoes, peeled and cubed
1 parsnip, sliced
2 red onions, sliced
2 garlic cloves, chopped
1 teaspoon dried thyme
½ teaspoon dried sage
Salt, pepper to taste
3 tablespoons balsamic vinegar

Directions:
Combine the vegetables in your crock pot. Sprinkle with
thyme, sage, salt and freshly ground pepper and cook on
low settings for 8 hours. When done, pour in the balsamic
vinegar and serve the vegetables warm or chilled.

Cheesy Cauliflower
Prep time: 10 minutes
Cook time: 6 ½ hours
Serves: 6

Are you a fan of cauliflower?! Then this is the recipe for you. It's rich, creamy and absolutely delicious.

What to expect

The cauliflower has a very mild taste and for that reason the one shining through this dish is the melted cheese and the subtle garlic aroma. The flavors combine perfectly to create this delicious dish.

Ingredients:
2 ½ pounds cauliflower, cut into florets
1 teaspoon garlic powder
½ teaspoon onion powder
1 ½ cups Alfredo sauce
2 cups grated Swiss cheese

Directions:
Combine the cauliflower with the garlic powder, onion powder and Alfredo sauce. Top with grated cheese then cover with its pot and cook on low settings for 6 ½ hours. Serve while still warm as a side dish for steak or even vegetables if you prefer a vegetarian menu.

Brown Rice and Zucchini Pilaf

Prep time: 15 minutes
Cook time: 7 ½ hours
Serves: 8

Pilaf is a rice dish that is usually very easy to make and this recipe makes no exception. It's a slow cooker recipe after all! But it turns out filling and flavorful, just what you want next to a steak or some roasted veggies.

<u>What to expect</u>

The brown rice has a stronger taste than any other kind of rice, but it's not overpowering at all. The brown rice is also healthier and has more nutrients than white rice so I highly recommend using it for this recipe.

Ingredients:
2 cups brown rice
5 cups vegetable stock
1 carrot, diced
1 cup edamame
1 cup green peas
1 shallot, finely chopped
Salt, pepper to taste

Directions:
Rinse the rice well then combine it with the stock, carrot, edamame, green peas and shallot in your crock pot. Season with salt and freshly ground pepper then cover with its lid and cook on low settings for 7 ½ hours. Serve the pilaf warm.

Slow Cooker Spiced Black Beans

Prep time: 10 minutes
Cook time: 4 ¼ hours
Serves: 6

Beans are a great source of fibers and protein, but they are also very filling and can easily be combined with steak or other kind of fried or roasted meat. The spices fit right in too!

<u>What to expect</u>

Unexpectedly, the black beans pair great with the spices. For more flavor, just before serving, crush part of the beans. This way the final dish will be creamier and the beans will release more flavor.

Ingredients:
2 cans black beans, drained
1 red onion, chopped
2 garlic cloves, chopped
1 jalapeno chile, seeded and chopped
½ teaspoon cumin powder
½ teaspoon ground ginger
½ teaspoon all-spice powder
1 teaspoon soy sauce
¼ cup vegetable stock
Salt, pepper to taste
2 tablespoons chopped cilantro

Directions:
Combine the beans with the red onion, garlic, chile and spices in your crock pot. Stir in the soy sauce and stock then season with salt and pepper to taste. Cover with its lid and

cook on high settings for 4 ¼ hours. When done, add the chopped cilantro and serve.

Cheesy Slow Cooker Potatoes

Prep time: 20 minutes
Cook time: 4 ½ hours
Serves: 6

As basic as potatoes may be, they can be used to make amazing dishes and this recipe is one of those rich, creamy and delicious dishes that you surely get to love in no time.

<u>What to expect</u>

The ingredient list is short and simple and the flavors are just as simple. However, the final taste is amazing and once again, this recipe shows that simplicity yield the best results.

Ingredients:
2 pounds red potatoes
½ cup heavy cream
½ cup milk
½ teaspoon dried thyme
½ teaspoon garlic powder
Salt, pepper to taste
2 cups grated Cheddar cheese

Directions:
Peel the potatoes and slice them finely. Place them in your crock pot and sprinkle with salt, pepper, thyme and garlic powder. Pour in the heavy cream and milk then top with grated cheese. Cook the potatoes on high settings for 4 ½ hours. Serve warm.

Roasted Squash

Prep time: 20 minutes
Cook time: 4 hours
Serves: 6

Squash may not be your first choice in terms of favorite vegetable, but it surely turns delicious into this recipe, creating a dish that can be paired with any main dish you can think of or even used as a base for a salad.

What to expect

Squash is rather sweet, but the herbs and olive oil balance it perfectly so the final dish is far from being sweet and falls more under the savory category. But it's delicious and definitely worth a try!

Ingredients:
1 acorn squash, peeled and cubed
¼ teaspoon cinnamon powder
1 teaspoon rosemary
1 teaspoon dried thyme
4 tablespoons olive oil
Salt, pepper to taste

Directions:
Combine the squash cubes with the cinnamon, rosemary, thyme, olive oil, salt and freshly ground pepper to taste. Place the squash in your crock pot and cook on high settings for 4 hours. Serve the squash warm.

Green Bean Cheesy Casserole

Prep time: 15 minutes
Cook time: 4 ½ hours
Serves: 6

Green beans make an excellent side dish if cooked right and paired with the right flavors. And this recipe has them all – lemon juice, the flavorful olive oil and plenty of salty Parmesan cheese. The perfect combination towards a delicious side dish.

<u>What to expect</u>

You will love the subtle tangy taste of this dish and the saltiness of the Parmesan. It's amazing how some basic green beans can turn into such a delicious side dish in this particular combination. Give it a try and you won't regret!

Ingredients:
2 pounds green beans, cut in smaller pieces
2 tablespoons lemon juice
4 tablespoons olive oil
½ cup cream of chicken soup
1 cup grated Parmesan cheese
Salt, pepper to taste

Directions:
Combine the green beans with the lemon juice, olive oil, chicken soup, salt and freshly ground pepper in your slow cooker. Top with grated Parmesan and cook on high settings for 4 ½ hours. Serve warm, while the cheese is still warm and melted.

Bacon Sauerkraut

Prep time: 15 minutes
Cook time: 4 ½ hours
Serves: 4

Sauerkraut is seriously underestimated nowadays, but it is very healthy and highly delicious so you should consider it in your cooking.

<u>What to expect</u>

The sauerkraut itself is tangy, salty and it does the best of teams with the smoky bacon. You will love the final results, I promise you!

Ingredients:
2 pounds shredded sauerkraut
1 teaspoon cumin powder
4 bacon slices, chopped
2 onions, finely chopped
1 teaspoon caraway seeds
1 cup beef broth
Salt, pepper to taste

Directions:
Mix the shredded sauerkraut with the cumin powder, bacon, onions, seeds and beef broth. Add salt and freshly ground pepper to taste then cook on high settings for 4 ½ hours. Serve warm as a side dish to steaks, although it's just as delicious served simple.

Soups and Stews

Slow Cooker Chili

Prep time: 15 minutes
Cook time: 9 ½ hours
Serves: 10

Who hasn't heard or tasted chili?! It's becoming a universal meal all around the globe lately, but none compares to the slow cooker one just because the taste is elevated and the making process is as minimalist as possible.

What to expect

This chili has an intense flavor and a nice spicy kick. Being cooked for such a long time, the flavor display is wide and the flavors themselves are intense and yet not overwhelming for your palate. It's a very enjoyable chili, perfectly balanced.

Ingredients:
1 pound ground beef
2 onion, finely chopped
2 celery stalks, chopped
2 red bell peppers, cored and diced
4 garlic cloves, chopped
2 cans tomato puree
1 can kidney beans, drained
1 can black beans, drained
1 can cannellini beans, drained
1 teaspoon chili powder
½ teaspoon hot paprika
1 teaspoon sweet paprika
1 teaspoon dried oregano

1 teaspoon dried basil
Salt, pepper to taste

Directions:
Combine the beef with the chopped vegetables. Add the tomato puree, beans and spices, as well as the dried herbs in your crock pot. Season with salt and freshly ground pepper. Cover the slow cooker with its lid and cook on low heat for 9 ½ hours. Serve the chili warm.

Creamy Bacon and Potato Soup

Prep time: 15 minutes
Cook time: 7 hours
Serves: 6-8

This recipe is so simple and yet so delicious. You would never think that such rustic, common ingredients can turn into something this tasty.

<u>What to expect</u>

It's a simple soup, the potatoes aren't very flavorful, but the bacon surely enhances the final taste. The coconut milk is there to thicken it and make it creamy, but it also adds a certain sweetness that creates an interesting contrast with the salty bacon.

Ingredients:
4 slices bacon, chopped
1 onion, chopped
1 can condensed chicken broth
2 cups water
6 large potatoes, peeled and cubed
½ teaspoon dried thyme
2 tablespoons cornstarch
2 cups coconut milk
Salt, pepper to taste

Directions:
Mix the bacon, onion, potatoes, thyme and cornstarch in a slow cooker. Pour in the chicken broth, water and coconut milk and then add salt and pepper to taste. Cook on low settings for 7 hours then serve the soup warm.

Lentil and Ham Soup

Prep time: 15 minutes
Cook time: 6 hours
Serves: 8

Who wouldn't love a delicious and rich bowl of soup after a long day at work?! This recipe is surely one of the best choices because it is filling and thick, but also very versatile.

<u>What to expect</u>

The ham is a nice addition to this soup, but you can remove it from the ingredient list easily and the soup will still be delicious, loaded with flavor, creamy and nutritious.

Ingredients:
1 ½ cups dried green lentils, rinsed
2 celery stalks, chopped
2 carrots, diced
1 onion, chopped
2 garlic cloves, chopped
1 cup diced ham
1 teaspoon dried basil
½ teaspoon all-spice powder
2 cups beef stock
2 cups water
Salt, pepper to taste

Directions:
Combine the lentils with the rest of the vegetables in your crock pot. Stir in the ham, basil and all-spice powder then pour in the beef stock and water. Add salt and pepper to taste and cook on low settings for 6 hours. Serve the soup warm.

Goulash

Prep time: 15 minutes
Cook time: 8 hours
Serves: 6-8

Having Hungarian roots, goulash is a very rich kind of stew that usually is being cooked on low heat for a longer period of time, allowing all those flavors to develop.

What to expect

It's a spicy dish, but that is what makes it special. A goulash without paprika is not a goulash for sure!

Ingredients:
2 pounds pork meat, cubed
2 onions, chopped
½ cup tomato puree
1 cup canned diced tomatoes
2 carrots, diced
1 celery stalk, chopped
1 ½ teaspoons smoked paprika
1 tablespoon sweet paprika
2 pounds red potatoes, peeled and cubed
Salt, pepper to taste
1 ½ cups vegetable or beef stock

Directions:
Mix the pork meat with the paprika and toss it around to evenly coat it then place it in your crock pot. Add the rest of the ingredients and season with salt and pepper to taste. Pour in the stock and cook on low settings for 8 hours. Serve it warm.

Sweet Potato Chicken Stew

Prep time: 20 minutes
Cook time: 6 ½ hours
Serves: 6-8

A warm stew that has a potato and chicken base to warm you up during the cold season especially.

<u>What to expect</u>

If you're a fan of sweet potatoes, you will love this recipe! The focus is actually not on the meat, but on the sweet potatoes, yielding a rather sweet dish, but delicious nonetheless.

Ingredients:
2 pounds sweet potatoes, peeled and cubed
2 zucchinis, sliced
1 red bell pepper, cored and sliced
2 chicken breasts, cubed
2 tablespoons olive oil
1 teaspoon dried rosemary
1 pinch cayenne pepper
½ cup chicken stock
Salt to taste

Directions:
Combine all the ingredients in your slow cooker. Season with salt to taste. Place the lid on and cook on high settings for 6 ½ hours or until the meat and veggies are tender. Serve right away.

Fish Chowder

Prep time: 15 minutes
Cook time: 6 ½ hours
Serves: 8

Don't avoid fish soups! You will be surprised to discover a whole new world of flavors, all based on that delicate, mild fish aroma.

<u>What to expect</u>

It's a light soup, but packed with subtle flavors to create a very soothing soup for your daily menus. It's very colorful, filling and nutritious as well.

Ingredients:
4 bacon slices, chopped
1 shallot, finely chopped
2 garlic cloves, chopped
6 cups chicken stock
4 cups fresh or frozen sweet corn kernels
3 potatoes, peeled and diced
1 celery stalk, chopped
1 pinch chili flakes
1 pound halibut, cubed
½ pound fresh shrimps, peeled and deveined
Salt, pepper to taste

Directions:
Combine the bacon with the shallot, garlic, chicken stock, corn, potatoes, celery and chili flakes in your slow cooker. Adjust the taste with salt and pepper. Cover with a lid and cook on low settings for 6 hours. Remove the lid and throw in the fish and shrimps. Cook 30 more minutes then serve the soup warm.

Lemony Salmon Soup

Prep time: 15 minutes
Cook time: 6 hours
Serves: 6

Salmon is a delicious kind of fish in any combination and
this soup is definitely one of them. The lemon juice cuts
down the aroma of the salmon and makes the soup lighter.

What to expect

The lemon makes the soup lighter and complements it
perfectly. The spinach added at the end is there to support
all the other flavors and make the soup as healthy as
possible.

Ingredients:
2 pound potatoes, peeled and cubed
3 salmon fillets, cubed
2 tablespoons olive oil
3 cups vegetable stock
1 cup water
½ lemon, juiced
1 teaspoon dried thyme
½ teaspoon dried sage
2 cups shredded spinach
Salt, pepper to taste

Directions:
Mix the potatoes with the olive oil, stock, water, dried herbs
and lemon juice in your crock pot. Cook on low settings for
5 hours. Remove the lid, throw in the salmon and spinach
and keep cooking for 1 more hour. Serve the soup warm.

Minestrone Soup

Prep time: 20 minutes
Cook time: 7 hours
Serves: 6-8

The Italian roots of this soup assures that this recipe is a real
success and it has a great Mediterranean aroma, refreshing
and absolutely delicious.

What to expect

Despite being such a rich and filling soup, it is actually
quite light and refreshing. The flavors are specific for the
Mediterranean Sea: olive oil, plenty of tomatoes, fresh
aromatic herbs and a touch of lemon juice.

Ingredients:
2 zucchinis, cubed
2 red potatoes, peeled and cubed
2 cups chopped green beans
1 cup green peas
3 ripe tomatoes, peeled and diced
Salt, pepper to taste
3 cups vegetable stock
2 tablespoons chopped parsley
2 tablespoons chopped cilantro
Salt, pepper to taste
½ lemon, juiced

Directions:
Combine the vegetables with the stock, salt and pepper in
your crock pot. Season with salt and pepper then cover the
pot with its lid. Cook the soup on low settings for 7 hours.
Just before serving add the chopped herbs. Serve the soup
warm, garnished with lemon juice.

Kids Favorites

Colorful Chicken Soup

Prep time: 20 minutes
Cook time: 8 hours
Serves: 6-8

Chicken soup has to be on the favorite list of your children!
Especially this delicious recipe that is loaded with plenty of
nutrients coming from all the fresh vegetables used.

<u>What to expect</u>

Is a very light soup, but it compensates through an intense
flavor and a soothing taste. The intense color of all the
ingredients is very appealing for kids.

Ingredients:
1 whole chicken, cut in smaller pieces
2 carrots, finely sliced
2 celery stalks, sliced
1 parsnip, finely sliced
4 potatoes, peeled and cubed
1 bay leaf
6 cups water
Salt, pepper to taste
4 tablespoons chopped parsley
1 tablespoon chopped cilantro
¼ cup white rice

Directions:
Combine the chicken with the vegetables, rice and water in
a crock pot. Add salt and pepper to taste and cook the soup
on low settings for 8 hours. Just before serving, stir in the

chopped herbs. Remove the meat off the bone before pouring in large bowls.

Bolognese Pasta

Prep time: 15 minutes
Cook time: 7 ½ hours
Serves: 4- 6

I recommend you to buy a fun kind of pasta for this dish.
How about alphabet pasta or maybe the animal shaped
kind?! Kids love fun food, don't forget that!

What to expect

Beef is a nutritious kind of meat, usually lean and flavorful.
You can use chicken or turkey though if your children don't
like beef. Either way, this sauce turns out delicious!

Ingredients:
2 pounds ground beef meat
2 large onions, finely chopped
1 celery stalk, chopped
1 carrot, finely grated
2 cups canned diced tomatoes
½ cup tomato paste
1 tablespoon brown sugar
Salt, pepper to taste
12 oz. gluten free pasta

Directions:
Mix the ground meat with the onions, celery, carrot, diced
tomatoes, tomato paste and brown sugar in your slow
cooker. Season with salt and freshly ground pepper and
cook the sauce on low settings for 7 ½ hours.
Cook the pasta in a large pot of boiling water for 8-10
minutes or until al dente. Serve the pasta topped with plenty
of Bolognese sauce.

Beef and Carrot Stew

Prep time: 15 minutes
Cook time: 8 hours
Serves: 8

The great thing about this stew is that your kids can dip some gluten free bread into the delicious gravy if they're not too fond into the meat itself. You can also freeze this stew for a quick lunch after they come to school. After all, microwave can be used by kids as well.

What to expect

It is a very kid friendly dish with mild flavors but plenty of nutrients. The flavor standing out however is the sweetness of the carrots, making this dish a real delight for children.

Ingredients:
1 ½ pound beef meat, cubed
2 tablespoons cornstarch
1 shallot, chopped
4 carrots, sliced
1 celery stalk, chopped
1 cup canned diced tomatoes
2 cups beef stock
Salt, pepper to taste

Directions:
Combine the meat with the cornstarch and mix well to evenly coat the meat. Place the meat cubes in your crock pot and stir in the shallot, celery stalk, carrots, tomatoes and beef stock. Add salt and pepper to taste and cook the stew on low settings for 8 hours. Serve the stew warm or freeze it in individual portions for later serving.

Macaroni and Cheese

Prep time: 15 minutes
Cook time: 3 ¼ hours
Serves: 6-8

Is there any kid that doesn't like mac'n'cheese?! I sure
don't know any, therefore this recipe is always a hit
amongst my children. It's always good to have a backup
recipe in case they don't like what I have for dinner.

What to expect

Basically, this dish is all about the gluten-free pasta and a
mix of cheeses that makes them absolutely delicious and
rich. You will love it too, not just your kids!

Ingredients:
10 oz. short gluten free pasta
2 cups milk
¼ cup butter, melted
2 tablespoons cornstarch
1 pinch salt
1 pinch nutmeg
2 eggs
1 ½ cups grated Cheddar cheese
1 cup shredded mozzarella

Directions:
Cook the pasta in a large pot of water until al dente. It
shouldn't take more than 8-10 minutes. Drain well and
place in your crock pot. Set aside.
Combine the milk with the cornstarch and melted butter in a
heavy saucepan. Cook until it begins to thicken then pour

over the pasta. Add the rest of the ingredients and cook on high settings for 3 ½ hours.
Serve warm.

Cheesy Spinach Frittata

Prep time: 15 minutes
Cook time: 5 ½ hours
Serves: 4-6

I know children don't quite like spinach, but this recipe rather hides it so they might actually ignore the green bits being too focused on the cheesy topping.

<u>What to expect</u>

It's a light dish, incredibly easy to make and yet very filling. Kids tend to love eggs so this is a good way to bring some variety into your children's menu.

Ingredients:
6 eggs
2 cups shredded spinach
2 sweet potatoes, peeled and cubed
½ teaspoon dried oregano
½ cup heavy cream
Salt, pepper to taste
1 ½ cups grated Cheddar cheese

Directions:
Beat the eggs with salt and pepper then stir in the remaining ingredients. Pour the mixture into your crock pot, top with cheese and cook on low settings for 5 1/5 hours. Serve right away.

Desserts

Fudgy Brownies

Prep time: 15 minutes
Cook time: 6 hours
Serves: 6-8

Brownies are a classic. They're impossible to not be liked with their fudgy texture and delicious taste. Plus, they are also very versatile and can be served with anything, from ice cream to whipped cream.

What to expect

Brownies surely have an intense chocolate taste and this recipe makes no exception. If you're a chocoholic, this is the recipe for you.

Ingredients:
¼ cup softened butter
½ cup dark chocolate chips, melted
2 eggs
½ cup sugar
½ cup applesauce
¼ cup warm water
1 teaspoon vanilla extract
1 pinch baking powder
1 cup brown rice flour
1 pinch salt

Directions:
Combine the soft butter with the melted chocolate. Stir in the eggs, sugar, applesauce, warm water and vanilla. Add the flour, baking powder and salt and give it a good mix.

Grease your crock pot with butter then pour the batter into your crock pot. Cook on low settings for 6 hours. Slice and serve the brownies simple or paired with your favorite toppings.

Raisin Stuffed Apples

Prep time: 15 minutes
Cook time: 3 hours
Serves: 6

Can it get simpler than this?! I say not! Just a few apples, raisins, brown sugar and cinnamon is all this recipe has! And it's absolutely delicious!

<u>What to expect</u>

Despite having just a few ingredients, the flavor display in this dish is amazing. The cinnamon blends perfectly with the tangy apples while the raisins add a natural sweetness and flavor of their own that works great with the caramel taste of the brown sugar.

Ingredients:
6 apples
½ cup raisins
¼ cup chopped walnuts
1 teaspoon cinnamon powder
1 pinch nutmeg
2 tablespoons brown sugar

Directions:
Carefully remove the core of the apples and place them all in your crock pot. Set aside.
Combine the raisins, walnuts, cinnamon powder, nutmeg and brown sugar. Spoon this mixture into each apple and cook the apples on high settings for 3 hours. They are better served slightly warm or chilled.

Cranberry Rice Pudding

Prep time: 10 minutes
Cook time: 3 hours
Serves: 6-8

Rice pudding always reminds me of childhood. It's creamy, filling and absolutely delicious, don't you agree with me?!

<u>What to expect</u>

I'm sure there will be no surprises with this dessert – you all remember it from childhood and it's one of the best and simplest desserts ever, fitted for both children and grown-ups. It's up to you to flavor it, the spices used in this recipe are just a suggestion.

Ingredients:
2 cups uncooked white rice, rinsed
2 cups evaporated milk
1 cup low fat milk
½ cup sugar
½ cup dried cranberries
2 tablespoons butter
1 vanilla bean, cut in half lengthwise
1 pinch salt

Directions:
Combine the uncooked rice with the evaporated milk and low fat milk in your crock pot. Stir in the sugar, cranberries, butter, vanilla bean and salt and cook on high settings for 3 hours. Serve the pudding warm.

Orange Cheesecake

Prep time: 15 minutes
Cook time: 5 ½ hours
Serves: 6-8

Despite many beliefs, a slow cooker can make excellent desserts, this cheesecake being one of the best examples. You will love the creamy texture and intense aroma.

What to expect

It's an amazing recipe that can easily be customize to fit your likings. This recipe asks for orange, but you can use lemons, strawberries, raspberries or even pears and apples.

Ingredients:
Crust:
1 ½ cups gluten free biscuits
½ cup melted butter
2 tablespoons powdered sugar
Filling:
16 oz. cream cheese
1 cup sour cream
3 eggs
2 tablespoons cream cheese
2 tablespoons orange zest
¼ cup fresh orange juice
1 pinch salt
½ cup sugar

Directions:
To make the crust, combine the biscuits with the powdered sugar in a food processor and pulse until ground. Add the melted butter and mix well then transfer the mixture in your crock pot and press it well on the bottom of the pot.

For the filling, combine all the ingredients in a bowl. Pour it in the crock pot and cook on high settings for 5 ½ hours. Let it cool down before slicing and serving.

Pear Cobbler

Prep time: 15 minutes
Cook time: 3 ½ hours
Serves: 6-8

Plenty of pears and a crunchy topping is what sets this dish apart of all the other slow cooker desserts. And trust me, it's delicious!

What to expect

The pears are quite delicate, but combined with a pinch of cinnamon and brown sugar they truly shine. The crunchy topping is there not just for the texture contrast, but also for a boosted aroma.

Ingredients:
Filling:
2 pounds pears, peeled and sliced
2 tablespoons brown sugar
½ teaspoon cinnamon powder
1 tablespoon dark rum
2 tablespoons lemon juice
Topping:
½ cup white rice flour
½ cup brown rice flour
1 cup buttermilk
2 tablespoons coconut oil
1 pinch salt
2 tablespoons brown sugar

Directions:
To make the filling, combine all the ingredients in your crock pot. Set aside.

For the topping, mix the rice flours with the buttermilk, coconut oil, salt and brown sugar. Spoon the batter over the pears and cook on high settings for 3 ½ hours. Serve slightly warm or chilled.

No Crust Pumpkin Pie

Prep time: 15 minutes
Cook time: 6 hours
Serves: 6-8

Pie takes a lot of time to make usually, but not this one.
Plus, there is no crust involved, just a creamy, rich pumpkin
filling.

<u>What to expect</u>

The flavors of this dessert are rather earthy, but absolutely
delicious. After all, it has cinnamon, nutmeg and vanilla – it
does sound delicious isn't it?!

Ingredients:
2 cups pumpkin puree
2 cups coconut milk
4 eggs
½ cup maple syrup
1 teaspoon vanilla extract
1 teaspoon cinnamon powder
1 pinch nutmeg
¼ teaspoon all-spice powder
¼ cup coconut flour
1 pinch salt

Directions:
Combine all the ingredients in your bowl and mix very well.
Grease your slow cooker then pour the mixture in. cook on
low settings for 6 hours. When done, let it cool down then
serve.

Apricot Coconut Crisp

Prep time: 15 minutes
Cook time: 2 1/2 hours
Serves: 6-8

The toasted coconut and crunchy granola topping is what makes this dessert special. You will surely love this amazing combination.

What to expect

The apricots are delicate and once baked they turn soft, creating a very nice contrast with the crunchy topping.

Ingredients:
2 pounds fresh apricots, pit removed
½ teaspoon cinnamon powder
1 pinch nutmeg
3 tablespoons brown sugar
1 cup coconut flakes
½ cup rice flour
¼ cup chopped almonds
4 tablespoons melted coconut oil
1 pinch salt

Directions:
Combine the apricots, cinnamon, nutmeg and brown sugar in your crock pot. Set aside.
Mix the coconut flakes with the rice flour, almonds, a pinch of salt and melted coconut oil and rub the mixture well.
Spread it over the apricots and bake in the slow cooker for 6 ½ hours on high settings.

Maple Poached Pears

Prep time: 15 minutes
Cook time: 3 ½ hours
Serves: 6

Poached pears is an exquisite dessert, fragrant and absolutely delicious. The pears turn tender and juicy, truly amazing if you think the ingredient list is so short and yet the final result is so good.

<u>What to expect</u>

For such a short prep time and just a few ingredients, this dessert turns out absolutely amazing. If you pair it with ice cream or whipped cream and even chocolate sauce, you've got yourself one of the best desserts ever.

Ingredients:
6 ripe pears
2 tablespoons lemon juice
½ cup fresh orange juice
1 teaspoon orange zest
1 teaspoon orange juice
¼ cup maple syrup
¼-inch piece of ginger, sliced

Directions:
Carefully peel the pears and remove their core. Place them in your crock pot and add the rest of the ingredients. Cook on high settings for 3 ½ hours and serve only when chilled.

Lemon Cornmeal Bread

Prep time: 15 minutes
Cook time: 6 hours
Serves: 6-8

A very rustic recipe that combines the cornmeal with lemon juice and lemon zest. Poppy seeds are added for a slight crunch and a subtle bitter taste to balance everything up.

<u>What to expect</u>

It's a rather rustic dessert, but delicious nonetheless! You will love the crunch of the poppy seeds and the tanginess of the lemon, all coming together into a dessert that can be served with ice cream fruit compote or a simple dollop of whipped cream.

Ingredients:
1 ½ cups white rice flour
2/3 cup cornmeal
2 tablespoons poppy seeds
1 teaspoon baking powder
1 pinch salt
½ cup maple syrup
½ cup butter, melted
3 eggs
4 tablespoons lemon juice
2 tablespoons lemon zest

Directions:
Combine the rice flour with the cornmeal, poppy seeds, baking powder and salt. Set aside.
Mix the melted butter with the maple syrup until well combined then stir in the eggs, lemon juice and lemon zest.
Stir in the rice flour mixture and give it a good mix.

Grease your crock pot with butter and pour the batter into the pot. Cook on low settings for 6 hours. Let it cool down then slice and serve.

Berry and Apple Compote

Prep time: 15 minutes
Cook time: 2 ½ hours
Serves: 4-6

This dessert certainly relies on the natural flavors of the fruits. You can serve it simple, you can top it with ice cream, gluten free biscuits or even freeze it into refreshing popsicles.

What to expect

This compote is highly fragrant and so refreshing, especially during those hot summer days. You will distinguish the flavors of every fruit use, but the final result is well balanced.

Ingredients:
4 green apples, peeled, cored and cubed
4 ripe pears, peeled and cubed
1 cup fresh strawberries
1 cup fresh blackberries
1 cup fresh raspberries
2 tablespoons lemon juice
1 cup fresh orange juice
½ cup water

Directions:
Combine the apples with the pears, lemon juice, orange juice and water in your slow cooker. Cook on high settings for 2 hours. Throw in the berries and finish cooking for 30 more minutes. When done, let it cool down then serve.

Conclusion

Having to turn to a gluten free diet is certainly not an easy change, especially since it means not only a different cooking in some cases, but also more care when buying ingredients and food. But you can make it easier by choosing the simplest path of all – slow cooking! Easy to make and no mixing or stirring involved – it sure sounds great, even for a novice in the kitchen!

Don't let that gluten intolerance define you! Learn to live with it rather than fight against it. It's not all that hard, and you certainly make your life easier through a healthy diet, careful meal planning and proper shopping. Plus, the biggest change is only when it comes to wheat products. You can still eat meat, eggs, fruits and vegetables so your options are limitless and, when the crockpot's involved, highly delicious!

Sofia

Thanks for reading!

A lot of love and care went into putting together these recipes and I do hope you enjoyed the book.

If you did, you could help support me most of all with an honest review on Amazon!

You would really make my day!

Simply head to Amazon.com and click *Your Account* followed by *Your Orders* to locate the book.

Printed in Great Britain
by Amazon

44759279R00050